AF342149

The journey to writing this book began when several mothers approached me to request that I teach a summer knitting class for children. Little did I know that my class would include more than 40 eager children ranging in age from 7 to 14. As **I began collecting my thoughts** on lesson plans and ideas, I found that the resources were few. So, being a designer, I decided to **plan my own fun projects.** **I asked some of the children** what they would like to make and **discovered** that most wanted to create things for family members or special friends. I remembered learning to knit as a 9-year-old and my delight in fashioning things for my loved ones. Even now, **the greatest joy of knitting** is sharing my handcrafted gifts with others. So, I have included several simple designs that children will enjoy knitting for themselves and others. I have also highlighted **teaching ideas and tips** that I have gathered from my experience. I hope that this book will be helpful as you instruct a new generation in this beloved craft. **May knitting bring you and your students as much joy as it has to me.**

I dedicate this book to my students. Their enthusiasm was a great inspiration and encouragement to me.

Kay Meadors

TABLE OF CONTENTS

This helpful guide for teachers and handbook for students will give you all the information you need to create an entertaining and educational class for children between ages 7 and 14. All you have to possess is knowledge of some basic knitting skills — we'll teach you the rest! The clearly written instructions do not include abbreviations — so they are easy for children to follow. Clever jingles will help students remember different stitches, and large diagrams can be photocopied for students to reference. Plus, fun and easy projects will help get your students excited about knitting.

So dig in — and prepare for an enjoyable, rewarding teaching experience!

TEACHER FAQ
(Frequently asked questions)

WHO WILL I TEACH?

If you don't already have in mind a group of potential students, try contacting one of the following organizations — local schools, church groups, Girl and Boy Scout Troops, or 4-H groups. Children who are at least 7 years old are the best age group to teach. Encourage both boys and girls to join your class — this book includes easy projects that are fun for all kids.

HOW BIG CAN THE CLASS BE?

Beginning classes can comfortably include eight to ten students, but first-time teachers may want to start with fewer students until they feel more confident. If more than ten children are interested in taking the class, consider enlisting someone to help you so that each student will have the individual help he or she may need. Or you might try splitting the group in two — one group could work on a different activity while the other group knits, then the groups could switch activities. This idea could work especially well if you have a willing helper who does not knit but is proficient at another skill.

WHERE SHOULD WE MEET?

If you are teaching a group that already meets regularly (such as a Scout Troop or a club), you can gather at the children's usual meeting place. You might also be able to hold class at a craft or yarn store, a private area in a local library, or a community center. Be sure the room you choose has good lighting and enough space for everyone to spread out a little while they work. Ideally, your meeting place should also be relatively quiet so the children can hear you easily and concentrate on their knitting.

HOW LONG SHOULD THE CLASS LAST?

Classes can consist of eight once-a-week sessions, but the amount of time you meet really depends on you and your students. If the children are older and pick up knitting quickly, you could possibly teach them the basics in four sessions.

As for the length of each session, you will probably need to adjust to your students' ages and attention spans, so be flexible. Too much class time can cause children (especially younger ones) to become bored and lose interest. You can start with about an hour, allowing more time in case it's needed. If the kids start getting restless, let them take a break.

You can give the following list of supplies to the children when they sign up for the class. Some children may already have access to a family member's needles and yarn. You might prefer to purchase the supplies for the rest of the students and allow them to reimburse you for the cost. This way, they will have exactly what they need. If you choose to do this, try buying a large skein of yarn and separating it into balls for the Bookmark, Wrist Band, or Napkin Ring. Also note that the knit projects in Lesson 3 can be made with leftover yarn from your projects.

If the students will be purchasing their own supplies, you might need to explain in more detail where to shop and what to buy. Suggest that they purchase 10" long needles rather than 14" needles because the shorter length makes them less awkward for little hands. Remind the children that many yarn companies use a standardized symbol for yarn weight *(see page 56)*. Medium/Worsted weight yarn will have a picture of a yarn ball with a number 4 and the word "medium."

Supplies:

Medium/Worsted weight yarn (for Bookmark, Wrist Band, Sweat Band, and Napkin Ring)
100% Cotton worsted weight yarn (for Coaster and Dishcloth)
10" straight knitting needles, size 8 (5 mm)
Scissors
Yarn needle
Tape measure (for future class)
Optional crochet hook, size H (5 mm) for dropped stitches and attaching fringe
Copy of this booklet, if students want to have written instructions for projects.

WHAT CAN I DO TO BE PREPARED?

To make sure you are prepared and organized, read all of the lessons in this book and memorize the Knit and Purl Jingles (the focus of learning the stitches).

Gather all of the materials you will need for the class. Remember — when you demonstrate how to knit, it will be easier for children to see what you are doing if you use large supplies. Try size 17 (12.75 mm) straight needles with bulky weight yarn or broomstick lace needles with macramé cord. Consider knitting the projects in Lessons 3 and 4 so you can show the class what they can look forward to making and exactly how their finished piece should look.

Leisure Arts grants permission to photocopy **only** the Knit and Purl Jingles, pages 23 and 29, to pass out to each student. **(It would be helpful if each student purchased a copy of this book so that they have the written projects available outside of class. Projects may not be copied for students to take home.)**

Don't forget to review all of your written materials shortly before the class, so that the information will be fresh in your mind.

WHAT ABOUT LESSONS & PROJECTS?

Each lesson in this book teaches children a knitting technique and has a small project children can make while practicing this technique. The projects are arranged in easy steps to acquire mastering each technique of stitches, decreases, increases, etc. Because every lesson builds on skills learned in the previous lesson, all should be studied in the order in which they are presented. Before long, the children will be able to make useful items for family, friends, and teachers, as well as themselves!

Advanced students may change the look of a project by using a different yarn. For example, the Scarf can be made with a soft, brushed acrylic yarn or in more than one color, to add stripes. Half the fun of knitting is using a favorite color or some of the fun yarns that are available.

RIGHT VS. LEFT HANDED STUDENTS?

Unlike some other skills, it doesn't matter for knitting if the student is right or left handed. Knitting is a two-handed process and may be slightly awkward at first but will quickly become easier with a little practice.

IS GAUGE IMPORTANT?

In the beginning projects, Lessons 1 through 5, gauge is not important. However, gauge is extremely important for sized projects, such as the Hat and the 2-Color Pullover. Students need to understand why gauge is important. If their gauge is too loose, they could run out of yarn or their project might be large enough to fit King Kong — but if their gauge is too tight, the project might be small enough for a mouse! Because everyone knits differently — loosely, tightly, or somewhere in between — the finished size can vary even when the knitters use the very same pattern, yarn, and needles. More information about gauge is given on page 57.

TEACHER TIPS

Once your class has started, begin working on a new lesson immediately so the children won't lose interest. Try following these three basic steps when you are teaching anything new:

Demonstrate with verbal explanation.
Have the students try it as you demonstrate again.
Walk around the room and watch them try it themselves.

Consider saving information that is not hands-on until later in the class. Students are more likely to stay enthusiastic if they are able to do something right away, rather than listening to someone for what seems to them a long period of time.

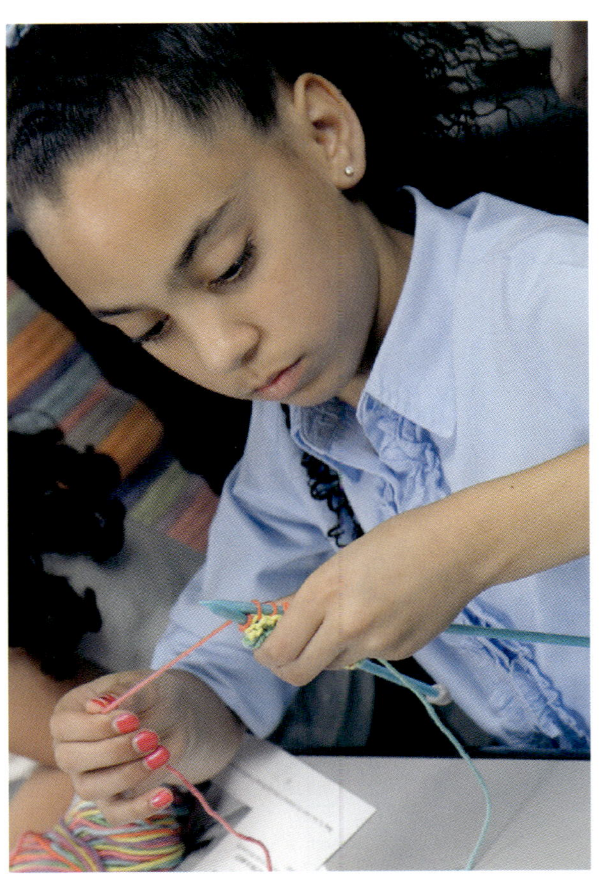

As time allows, give each of your students some individual attention. Some children may try to demand your constant attention. Encourage them, but politely pair them up with another student who has a better understanding of the lesson so that you are free to help all of the children.

If you notice that a student's attention is straying during practice time, give him or her a break. Let the child do the finger exercises shown on page 15, get a drink of water, or walk around the room to see how everyone else is doing for a few minutes — then encourage him or her to try knitting again. As a special treat, you can schedule a class at the lunch hour and break for pizza!

As the students learn at their own rate, some will naturally work faster than others. Remind the children that this is normal. The important thing is that they are working at a speed that is comfortable for them. If you discover that some students are working so quickly that they are becoming bored with what they have already learned, feel free to begin teaching them more advanced skills.

Remember — be flexible and keep it simple. Don't feel pressured to teach everything in one class. Teach at a pace that works for your students. Classes can easily continue from four to eight sessions.

THE FIRST SESSION

In most cases, students will not get to class all at the same time. Keep finished projects, yarn, books, and knitting tools on hand for children to look at while they wait for everyone to arrive. Be enthusiastic about the materials — this will get them interested in and excited about what they are going to learn. Chat with students. Begin learning their names and establish a rapport if you don't already know them.

Just before class starts, pass out copies of the Knit and Purl Jingles, pages 23 and 29. Find out if anyone already knows how to knit. Separate the students by their skill level. During practice time, review their skills to make sure they really can knit.

When you are ready to start the class, immediately begin with Lesson 1, Making a Slip Knot. Try to keep the class moving — ideally, you should finish Lessons 1-3 in your first session.

As you begin teaching the knit stitch, it
is important that the children can see what
you are doing. Try sitting in a chair or on the
floor with the students standing behind you.
Demonstrate the knit stitch using large straight
knitting needles and bulky yarn or broomstick
lace needles and macramé cord. Begin teaching
your students the knit jingle. Demonstrate the
stitch again, repeating the jingle and the verbal
explanation.

After you have reviewed the knit stitch several
times, allow students return to their seats. Walk
around the room, carrying your knitting with
you so you can demonstrate again as needed.
Encourage the children to reference the jingles
and help each other.

End the class by praising your students for their efforts and telling them what they can look forward to learning next week. The more enthusiastic you are about the upcoming lesson, the more excited the children will be!

Kids just love to have fun — and who doesn't? Above all, remember that knitting **should** be fun and do your best to make it fun for your students.

Learning a new skill isn't always easy. While knitting may be second nature to you now, remember that it once was new, exciting, and awkward. Expect that learning to knit will be easier for certain students than it will for others. Some children may even get frustrated. All of your students will need lots of encouragement and praise.

Walk around the class to spot anyone who might not understand. **Encourage students to raise their hand** if they need you. Some children are sensitive and may be embarrassed to ask for assistance, so be ready to help them without drawing unnecessary attention.

The children's first projects may be lop-sided — reassure them that it's okay. Think back … your early projects were probably lop-sided, too! Don't worry if students drop a stitch or even "find" one. As they are just beginning to learn, don't have them rip out mistakes, just work around them. Later, when they have more confidence, you can show them how easy it is to fix a mistake. *(See Dropped Stitches, page 58.)* The important thing is the new skill that they are learning and enjoying. Learning every method of holding yarn and making stitches perfectly isn't as important as being comfortable. They can always work on the methods later. Perfection and even stitches will come with practice.

Don't fret if it turns out that one or two children just don't get it. If you make the class a positive experience, they might try knitting again when they are a little older. Above all, remember to be patient.

PRACTICE

Practice? Why practice?

It's easier for anyone to learn a new skill if they practice it — then they don't have a chance to forget all that they've learned! If the children haven't finished their project by the end of the class, they should work on it and bring it to the next session ready to bind off. If they did finish, get them started on something small and fun that they can practice on. Emphasize that the more they knit, the more comfortable they will be holding the needles and making the stitches. Soon they'll be old pros!

WHERE CAN WE GET MORE SMALL, FUN PROJECTS?

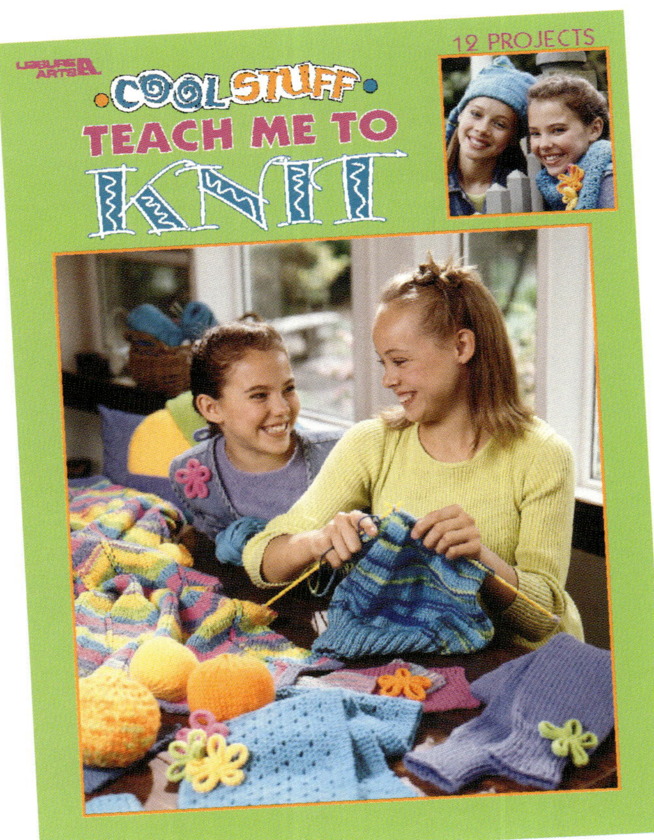

Our leaflet #3322, "Cool Stuff Teach Me To Knit" has lots of projects for kids and all the information they might need for reference. In addition, "10-20-30 Minutes to Learn to Knit" (leaflet #3231) includes patterns for two dishcloths, slippers, a baby toy, a mitten hand puppet, and more. Remember — it is very important that the projects the children choose are not too difficult, so that they can finish them without getting discouraged. They may need help choosing additional projects geared to their skill level and their interests. Look for books with simple projects to find something your students will be excited about making.

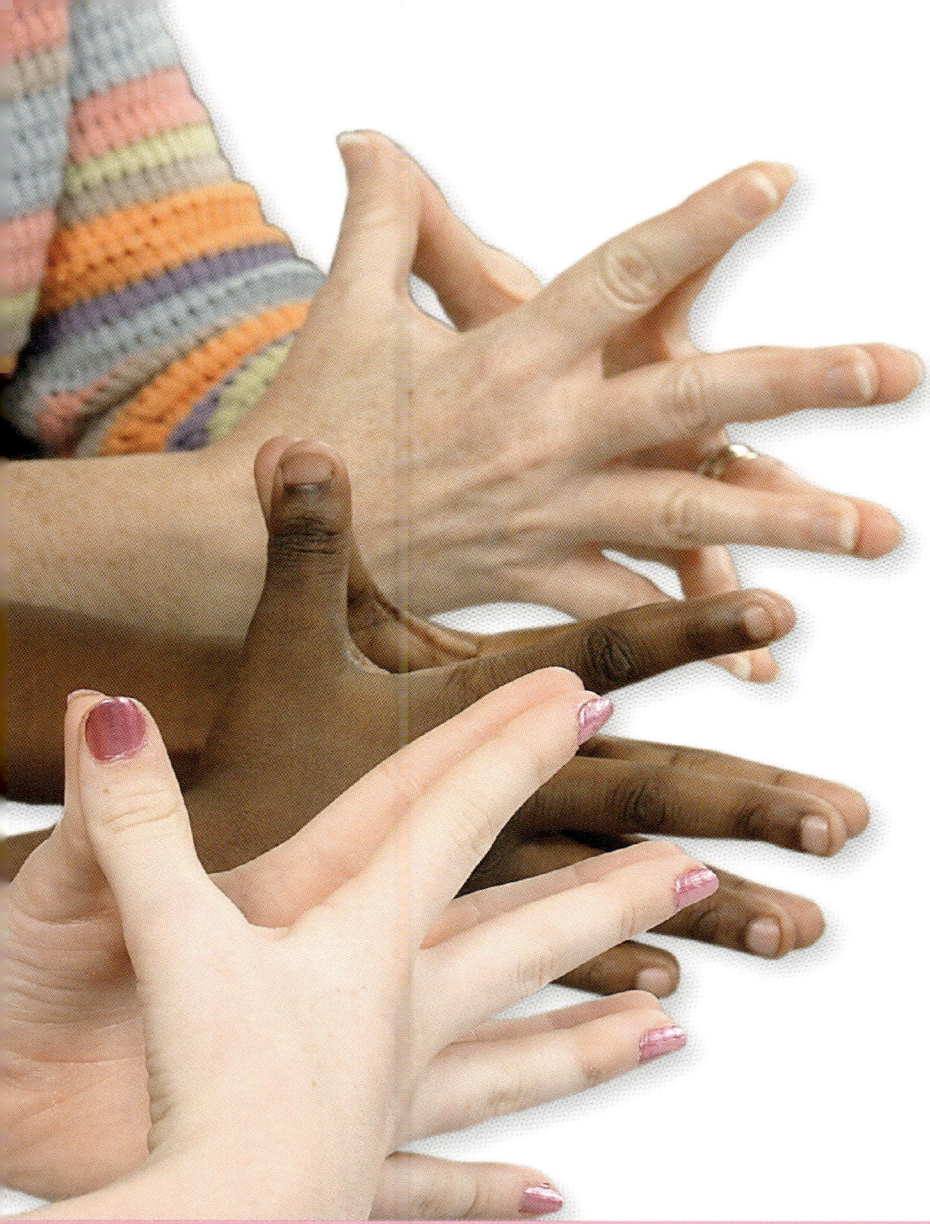

FINGER EXERCISES

Finger exercises are great for children. The exercises will prevent cramping, relieve tension, and give them a break from knitting if they start to get bored or distracted.

Try the exercises shown below:

Finger Stretch

1. Spread fingers out, then move them together again.
2. Repeat.

Spider Push-Ups

1. Touch the fingertips of both hands together.
2. Push fingers out, straightening knuckles.
3. Move fingers together until they touch again.
4. Repeat.

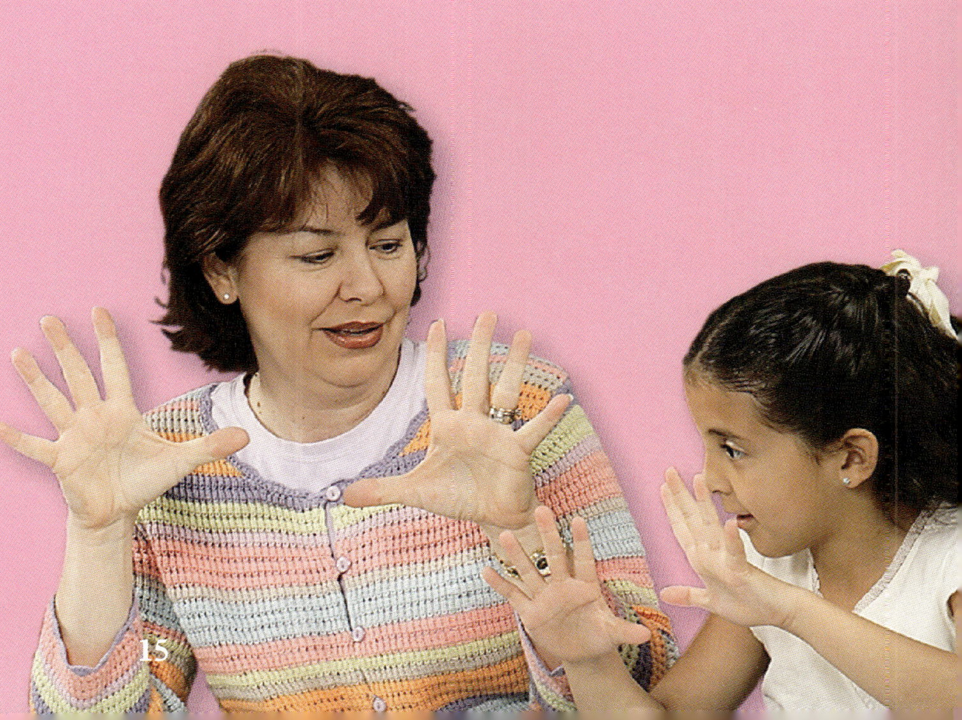

LESSON 1: SLIP KNOT

 Let the students attempt to make a few slip knots, but don't spend too much time on knots.

Let's start by learning how to make a slip knot to put on your needle. This is the first step you'll do in all the knit projects you make.

Step 1: With your right hand, pick up the end of the yarn and place it behind your left hand, then across your thumb and palm. Hold the yarn end over the working yarn (which is the yarn coming from the skein). Don't let go of the yarn *(Fig. 1a)*.

Fig. 1a

Fig. 1b

Fig. 1d

Fig. 1c

Practice making a **slip knot** until you are **comfortable** making one, then go to Step 4, page 18.

Step 4: Place the loop on your needle with the working yarn closest to your right hand. Pull the working yarn to tighten it around the needle ***(Fig. 1e)***. Keep the loop loose enough to slide easily across the shaft of the needle. The slip knot counts as your first cast on stitch.

Fig. 1e

To "un-do" the knot, just slip the needle out of the loop and pull on both ends of the yarn!

To begin knitting, you'll need to cast on a beginning number of stitches onto one needle, so go to Lesson 2: Thumb Cast On.

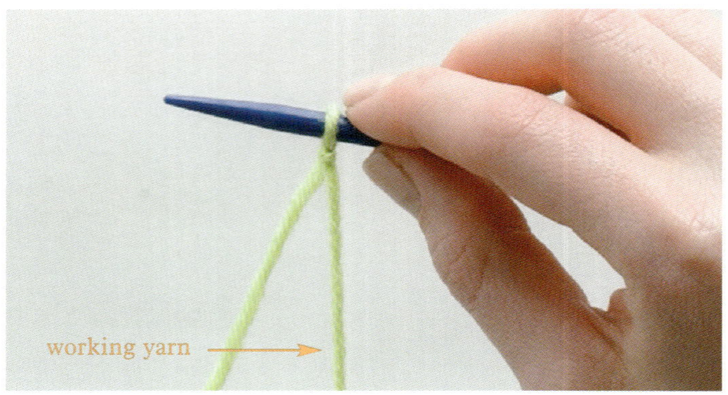

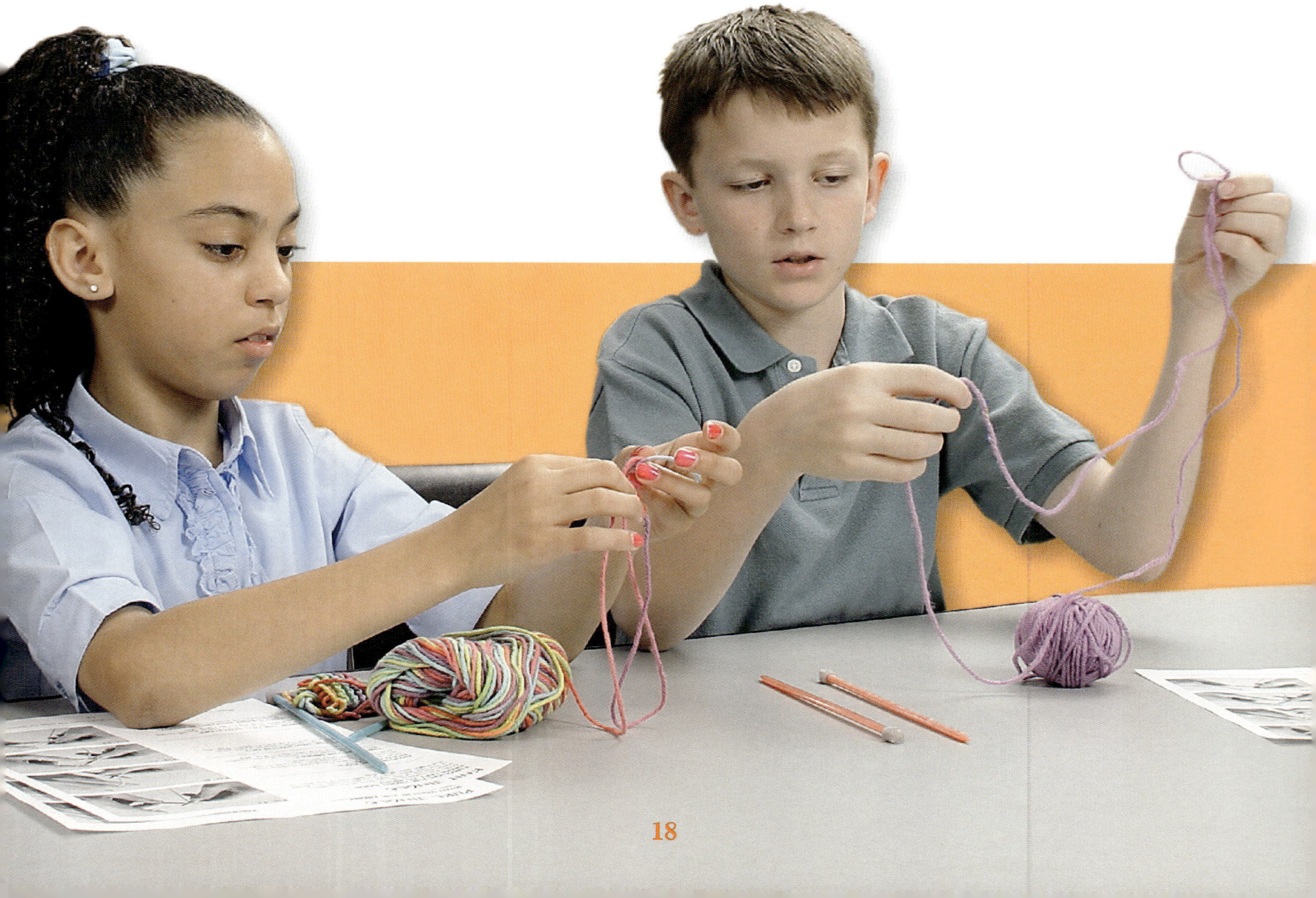

LESSON 2: THUMB CAST ON

"Cast on" is a term used to describe placing a beginning number of stitches on the needle.

Step 1: Pull enough yarn from the skein to match the length of your arm. Make a slip knot at that point *(see pages 16 - 18)*, pulling gently on both yarn ends to tighten the stitch on the needle (remember, this counts as your first cast on stitch).

Step 2: Hold the needle with the stitch on it in your right hand; place the working yarn over your index finger and grip the yarn in your palm with your ring finger and little finger *(Fig. 2a)*.

Fig. 2a

Step 3: Hold the short end of the yarn in the palm of your left hand and loop it from front to back around your thumb *(Fig. 2b)*.

Fig. 2b

Step 4: Slide the tip of the needle upwards through the yarn loop on your left thumb *(**Fig. 2c**)*.

Fig. 2c

Step 5: Take the working yarn over the tip of the needle with your right index finger *(**Fig. 2d**)*.

Fig. 2d

Step 6: Pull the yarn and needle down through the loop on your thumb *(**Fig. 2e**)*. This forms a stitch.

Fig. 2e

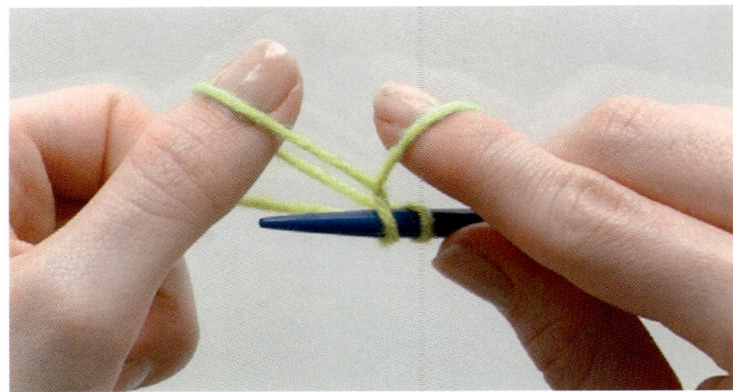

Step 7: Slip your thumb out of the loop. Gently pull the loop to tighten the new stitch on the needle *(**Fig. 2f**)*. Catch the end of the yarn to make a new loop on your thumb.

Fig. 2f

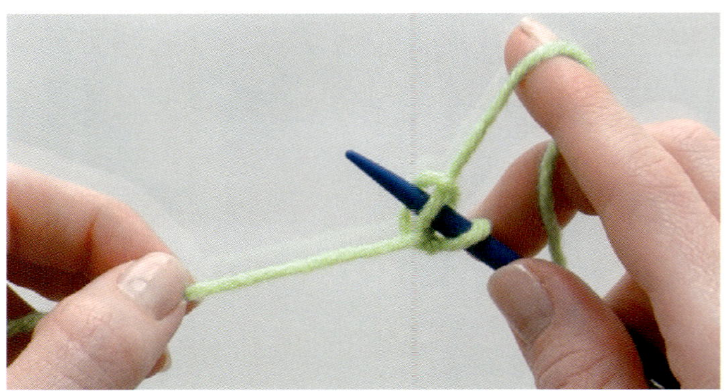

Repeat Steps 4-7 for each new stitch.

for casting on, allow about 1" (2.5 cm) of yarn for each stitch you cast on and place your slip knot there. When you work with thinner yarns, it will take slightly less than 1" (2.5 cm) per stitch while heavier yarns will take a little more.

Make your cast on stitches snug, but not too tight. The tip of the needle should easily slide into each stitch as you work the first row of knitting.

You may cut the yarn end shorter after you have cast on all your stitches, **but make sure you leave** enough (at least as long as your hand) so you can weave it in **later** to hide the end. If the yarn end is going to **be** used later to sew a seam, leave an arm's **length,** roll it into a ball, and pin it to the bottom **of** your project until you need it.

LESSON 3: KNIT STITCH & BIND OFF

Teacher's Note: Have each child choose one of the four easy projects in this lesson that he or she would like to make while learning and practicing how to make a knit stitch. The Bookmark doesn't even require any sewing.

HOLDING THE YARN

Before learning the knit stitch, practice winding the yarn around your right hand. With your left hand, pass the working yarn over the little finger of your right hand, under your two middle fingers, and over your index finger *(Fig. 3)*. This will feel awkward at first, but controlling the yarn in this way will help you make your stitches the same size.

Fig. 3

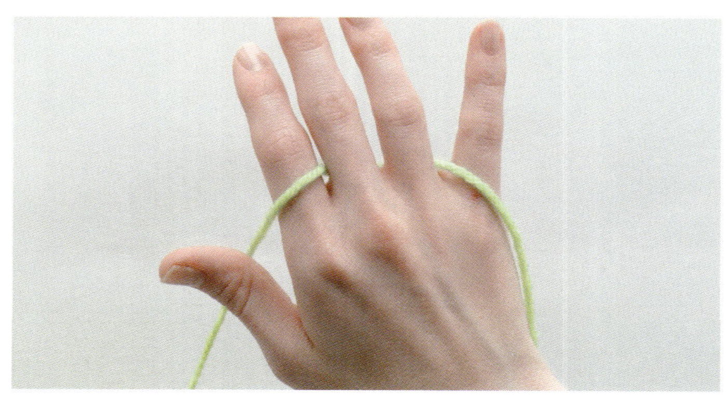

BOOKMARK, WRIST BAND, SWEAT BAND, OR NAPKIN RING

MATERIALS
Medium/Worsted Weight Yarn:
  Bookmark, Wrist Band, & Napkin Ring:
    10 yards (9 meters) **each** project
  Sweat Band: 20 to 25 yards
    (18.5 to 23 meters)
Straight knitting needles, size 8 (5 mm)
Yarn needle
For Napkin Ring Only: plastic canvas -
  $1^{1}/_{2}$"w x $5^{1}/_{2}$"h (4 cm x 14 cm) piece **each**

Cast on 6 stitches.

Hold the needle with the cast on stitches in your left hand and the empty needle in your right hand.

Row 1: Follow the Knit Jingle, page 23, for each **stitch across** the needle.

Teacher's Note: Have the children memorize the jingle as you explain how to make a knit stitch. Have them repeat the jingle for each stitch they make until they understand how to make it.

Knit each stitch across every row until piece is 6" (15 cm) long for Bookmark, $^{1}/_{2}$" (12 mm) less than **your wris**t measurement for Wrist Band, $^{1}/_{2}$" (12 mm) less than your head measurement for the **Sweat Ban**d, or $5^{1}/_{2}$" (14 cm) long for Napkin Ring. (See the handy ruler on page 60.) After you have **complete**d the length needed for your project, it is **time to lea**rn how to bind off.

Instructions continued on page 24.

KNIT JINGLE

THROUGH THE FRONT DOOR
FROM LEFT TO RIGHT
(With the working yarn in back of the needles, insert the tip of the right needle through the **front** of the first stitch from the **left** side of the stitch to the **right** side.) *(Fig. 4a)*

Fig. 4a

AROUND THE BACK
HOLD ON TIGHT
(With your right hand, bring your working yarn around the back, making sure you hold on tight to both needles with your left hand.)

THROUGH THE MIDDLE
(Bring the working yarn between the two needles; this loop will become your new stitch.) *(Fig. 4b)*

Fig. 4b

BRING THE NEW STITCH OUT
(With the right needle, bring your new stitch toward you and out of the old stitch.) *(Fig. 4c)*

Fig. 4c

DROP THE OLD STITCH OFF
(Slide the old stitch to the end of the left needle and drop it off the needle.) *(Fig. 4d)*

THAT'S WHAT KNITTING IS ABOUT!
(Repeat the Knit Jingle for each stitch across the left needle. Once all the stitches are on the right needle, switch the needle to your left hand and begin again.)

Fig. 4d

Note: You have Leisure Arts' permission to photocopy this page for teaching purposes only.

KNIT BIND OFF

Step 1: Knit two stitches.

Step 2: Holding the yarn **behind** the work, insert the left needle into the first stitch on the right needle. Pull the first stitch over the second stitch and off the right needle *(Fig. 5a)*. One stitch has been bound off and one stitch remains on your right needle.

Fig. 5a

Step 3: Knit the next stitch.

Repeat Steps 2 and 3 to bind off all the stitches until there is only one stitch left on your right needle, ending with Step 2.

Step 4: To lock the last stitch, cut your working yarn, leaving a long yarn end for sewing, about 12" (30.5 cm). Bring the cut yarn through the last stitch *(Fig. 5b)*, pulling the yarn end to tighten.

Fig. 5b

FINISHING

Bookmark: Weave in both yarn ends
(Fig. 7, page 26).

Wrist and Sweat Bands: Whipstitch ends of
knit piece together *(Fig. 6, page 26)*. Weave
in both yarn ends *(Fig. 7, page 26)*.

Napkin Ring: Sew the short ends of the
plastic canvas strip together forming a ring.
Whipstitch ends of knit piece together
(Fig. 6, page 26).
Slip the plastic canvas ring inside the
Napkin Ring and sew through the edges
along both of the long edges. Weave in both
yarn ends *(Fig. 7, page 26)*.

WHIPSTITCH

Thread a yarn needle with the long end left after binding off. Fold knit piece in half. Holding ends together, work whipstitch as follows: insert the needle from **back** to **front** in stitch on both ends *(Fig. 6)* and pull the yarn through. Repeat for each stitch across.

Fig. 6

WEAVING IN YARN ENDS

Thread the yarn needle with one of the yarn ends. Weave the yarn **loosely** through several stitches, then double back and weave the yarn through several stitches in the opposite direction *(Fig. 7)*. Clip the end close to the stitches.

Fig. 7

LESSON 4: PURL STITCH

Teacher's Note: The Coaster and the Dishcloth are small projects to make while learning how to make a purl stitch.

COASTER
MATERIALS

Medium/Worsted Weight Cotton Yarn:
  20 yards (18.5 meters) **each**
Straight knitting needles, size 8 (5 mm)
Stitch markers - 2
Plastic canvas - approximately 5" (12.5 cm)
  square for **each** Coaster
Yarn needle

Cast on 20 stitches.

Hold the needle with the cast on stitches in your left hand and the empty needle in your right hand.

Row 1: Follow the Purl Jingle, page 29, for each stitch across the needle.

Teacher's Note: Have the children memorize the jingle as you explain how to make a purl stitch, just as they did for the knit stitch. Have them repeat the jingle for each stitch they make until they understand how to make it.

Rows 2-8: Purl each stitch across the row. (You should have 4 ridges.)

Stitch markers are used to let you know that the pattern you are knitting is about to change. When you come to a marker on the left needle, slip it to the right needle and work the next stitches as indicated in the pattern. You can used purchased markers or a short piece of yarn tied snugly around the needle.

Row 9 (Right side): Purl 5 stitches, place a stitch marker on the right needle, knit 10 stitches, place a stitch marker on the right needle, purl the last 5 stitches.

Instructions continued on page 30.

PURL JINGLE

Fig. 8a

WITH YARN IN THE FRONT
(Your yarn will always start in the front of your work when purling.)

GO FROM RIGHT FRONT TO LEFT
(Insert the tip of the right needle through the first stitch from the **right** side of the stitch to the **left** side, keeping the right needle in front of the left needle.) *(Fig. 8a)*

Fig. 8b

BRING THE YARN OVER AND AROUND
(With your right hand, bring your working yarn over the right needle and back around to where you started, holding both needles with your left hand.) *(Fig. 8b)*

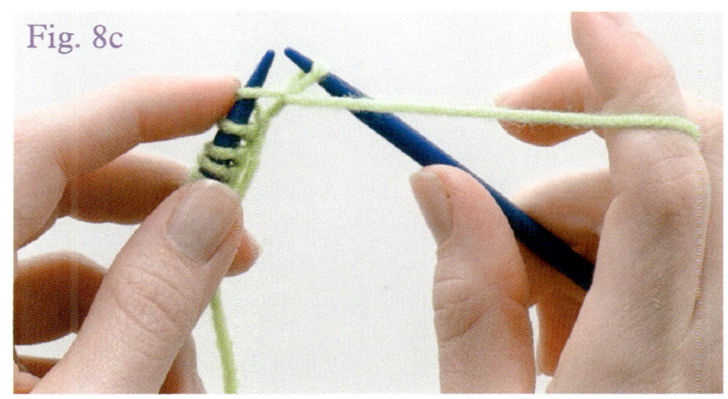

Fig. 8c

TRY IT YOURSELF
THROUGH THE MIDDLE OUT THE BACK
BRING THE NEW STITCH THRU
(Try it: With the right needle, bring your new stitch away from you and out through the old stitch.) *(Fig. 8c)*

Fig. 8d

DROP THE OLD STITCH OFF
(Slide the old stitch to the end of the left needle and drop it off the needle.) *(Fig. 8d)*

NOW YOU'RE PURLING, TOO!
(Repeat the Purl Jingle for each stitch across the left needle. Once all the stitches are on the right needle, switch the needle to your left hand and begin again.)

Note: You have Leisure Arts' permission to photocopy this page for teaching purposes only.

Row 10: Purl each stitch across the row, slipping the markers.

Row 11: Purl each stitch across to the first marker, knit each stitch across to the next marker, purl the last 5 sts.

Rows 12-25: Repeat Rows 10 and 11, 7 times, removing both markers on Row 25.

Rows 26-33: Purl each stitch across the row.

After you have completed Row 33, it is time to learn the purl bind off.

PURL BIND OFF
Step 1: Purl two stitches.

Step 2: Holding the yarn in **front** of the work, insert the left needle into the first stitch on the right needle. Pull the first stitch over the second stitch and off the right needle, same as you did for the Knit Bind Off, page 24. One stitch has been bound off and one stitch remains on your right needle.

Step 3: Purl the next stitch.

Repeat Steps 2 and 3 to bind off all the stitches until there is only one stitch left on your right needle, ending with Step 2.

Step 4: Cut your working yarn about 30" (76 cm) from the Coaster. Bring the cut yarn through the last stitch (**Fig. 5b, page 24**), pulling the yarn end to tighten.

FINISHING
Cut a plastic canvas square the same size as your Coaster. Thread the yarn needle with the long end left after binding off and sew the Coaster to the plastic canvas square at each edge. Weave in the yarn ends (**Fig. 7, page 26**).

DISHCLOTH

MATERIALS

Medium/Worsted Weight Cotton Yarn:
 1½ ounces, 70 yards
  (40 grams, 64 meters)
Straight knitting needles, size 8 (5 mm)
Stitch marker
Yarn needle

Cast on 35 stitches.

Rows 1-6: Knit each stitch across the row.

Row 7: Knit 3 stitches, place a stitch marker on the right needle, purl each stitch across until there are only 3 stitches left on the left needle, place a stitch marker on the right needle, knit the last 3 stitches.

Row 8 (Right side): Knit each stitch across the row, slipping the markers.

Row 9: Knit 3 stitches, purl each stitch across to the next marker, knit the last 3 stitches.

Rows 10-19: Repeat Rows 8 and 9, 5 times.

Rows 20-26: Knit each stitch across the row, slipping the markers.

Row 27: Knit 3 stitches, purl each stitch across to the next marker, knit the last 3 stitches.

Rows 28-39: Repeat Rows 8 and 9, 6 times.

Rows 40-46: Knit each stitch across the row, slipping the markers.

Row 47: Knit 3 stitches, purl each stitch across to the next marker, knit the last 3 stitches.

Rows 48-59: Repeat Rows 8 and 9, 6 times, removing both markers on Row 59.

Rows 60-65: Knit each stitch across the row.

Bind off all stitches in **knit**.

Weave in the yarn ends.

LESSON 5: INCREASING & DECREASING

Teacher's Note: The knit increase in this lesson uses one stitch to make two stitches and is formed by working into the front and into the back of the same stitch. You will have two stitches on the right needle for the one stitch worked off the left needle.

JUGGLING BALL

MATERIALS

Medium/Worsted Weight Cotton Yarn:
21 yards (19 meters) **each**
Straight knitting needles, size 8 (5 mm)
Knee high stocking - one for **each** Ball
2/3 cup of uncooked rice for **each** Ball
Yarn needle

BODY

Cast on 9 stitches.

ROW 1 (Increase row)
Step 1: To make a knit increase, knit the first stitch but do **not** slip the old stitch off the left needle **(Fig. 9a)**.

Fig. 9a

Step 2: Instead, insert the right needle into the **back** loop of the **same** stitch **(Fig. 9b)** and knit it, then slip the old stitch off the left needle. You now have two stitches on your right needle and have made your first knit increase.

Fig. 9b

Step 3: Repeat Steps 1 and 2 to increase in each remaining stitch across the row: you will now have 18 stitches.

Instructions continued on page 34.

Row 2: Purl each stitch across the row.

Row 3 (Right side)**:** Work the knit increase in each stitch across the row: you will now have 36 stitches.

Row 4: Purl each stitch across the row.

Row 5: Knit each stitch across the row.

Row 6: Purl each stitch across the row.

Rows 7-10: Knit each stitch across the row.

Teacher's Note: Have the children count the number of stitches after they finish each row. This is a good habit for them to form.

Row 11: Purl each stitch across the row.

Row 12: Knit each stitch across the row.

Row 13: Purl each stitch across the row.

Rows 14-17: Knit each stitch across the row.

Row 18: Purl each stitch across the row.

Row 19: Knit each stitch across the row.

Row 20: Purl each stitch across the row.

ROW 21 (Decrease row)
Step 1: To decrease, insert the right needle into the **front** of the first two stitches on the left needle as if to **knit** *(Fig. 10a)*.

Fig. 10a

Step 2: Knit the two stitches together as if they were one stitch *(Fig. 10b)*. *Note:* Each decrease subtracts one stitch from the amount of stitches on your needle.

Fig. 10b

Step 3: Knit 2 stitches together across the row: you will now have 18 stitches.

Instructions continued on page 36.

Row 22: Purl each stitch across the row.

Row 23: Knit 2 stitches together across the row: you will now have 9 stitches.

Cut the working yarn, leaving a long end for sewing.

Thread a yarn needle with the long end and insert it through the 9 stitches on the needle *(Fig. 11)*, removing the knitting needle. Pull the yarn tightly to close, then make a knot to secure the yarn. Do not remove the yarn needle and do not cut the yarn.

Fig. 11

FINISHING

Pour the rice into the toe of the knee high. **Twist** the knee high to close and **pull** the unused part over the rice ball; **repeat as many times as needed** to use up as much of the knee high as possible, then either knot the remaining part or sew the top closed.

Weave the seam of the knit Ball halfway closed *(Fig. 12)*. Place the rice ball inside the knit Ball and finish weaving the seam the rest of the way. Weave the yarn end through the beginning 9 stitches; pull the yarn tightly to close, then make a knot to secure the yarn. **Insert the needle** into the Ball and push it out to the other side. **Cut the yarn end close** to the Ball.

WEAVING SEAMS

With the **right** side of both pieces facing you and the edges lined up, sew through **both** sides once to secure the seam. Insert the needle under the bar between the first and second stitches on the row and pull the yarn through *(Fig. 12)*. Insert the needle under the next bar on the second side. Repeat from side to side, being careful to line up the rows and pulling the seam closed as you work.

Fig. 12

LESSON 6: YARN OVERS

Teacher's Note: This Lap Throw presents opportunities to learn several new things in addition to the yarn over pattern. Your students will be using a larger size circular needle, bulky yarn, and also learning about gauge.

LAP THROW
Finished Size: 36" x 48" (91.5 cm x 122 cm)

MATERIALS
Super Bulky Weight Yarn:
   32 ounces, 980 yards
      (910 grams, 896 meters)
29" (73.5 cm) Circular needle, size 11 (8 mm) **or**
   size needed for gauge *(see Gauge, page 57)*
Stitch markers - 2
Yarn needle

GAUGE: In pattern,
     12 sts and 20 rows = 4" (10 cm)

Cast on 108 sts.

Rows 1-7: Knit each stitch across the row.

ROW 8 (Right side)
Step 1: Knit 4, place a stitch marker on the right needle.

Step 2: To make a yarn over, bring the yarn forward between the needles and back over the top of the right needle so that it's in position to knit the next stitch *(Fig. 13)*.

Fig. 13

Note: When you see a ★ (star) in the instructions, it means that you should work only the instructions following the first ★, and repeat those instructions across the row until the number of stitches indicated are left, then work the instructions for the last stitches *(see Symbols and Terms, page 56)*.

Step 3: Knit 2 stitches together (*Figs. 10a & b, page 35*), ★ yarn over, knit 2 stitches together; repeat from ★ across to the last 4 stitches, place a stitch marker on the right needle, knit the last 4 stitches: You'll still have 108 sts.

Note: On the row following a yarn over, be careful to keep the yarn over on the needle and treat it as a stitch by knitting it (*Figs. 14a and b*).

Fig. 14a

Fig. 14b

Rows 9 and 10: Knit each stitch across the row, slipping the markers.

Row 11: Knit each stitch across to the first marker, purl each stitch across to the next marker, knit the last 4 stitches.

Rows 12 and 13: Knit each stitch across the row, slipping the markers.

Row 14: Knit each stitch across to the first marker, ★ knit 2 stitches together, yarn over; repeat from ★ across to the next marker, knit the last 4 stitches.

Rows 15 and 16: Knit each stitch across the row, slipping the markers.

Row 17: Knit each stitch across to the first marker, purl each stitch across to the next marker, knit the last 4 stitches.

Rows 18 and 19: Knit each stitch across the row, slipping the markers.

Row 20: Knit each stitch across to the first marker, ★ yarn over, knit 2 stitches together; repeat from ★ across to the next marker, knit the last 4 stitches.

Rows 21-230: Repeat Rows 9-20, 17 times; then repeat Rows 9-14 once **more**, removing both markers on Row 230.

Rows 231-237: Knit each stitch across the row.

Bind off all stitches in **knit**.

Weave in the yarn ends.

Always start a new ball or skein at the beginning of a row, never in the middle (*Fig. 15*). Cut the yarn, leaving an end at least as long as your hand. Tie it to the new yarn with a single knot that is not too tight. You will untie it when you weave in the yarn ends. The ends can be woven into the edge or in the back of the work.

Fig. 15

BONUS PROJECTS

Teacher's Note: The following projects will build on the skills your students learned in Lessons 1 through 6 by adding the finishing techniques of fringe, tassels, twisted cords, and pom-poms.

Finished Size: 16" wide x 12" high (40.5 cm x 30.5 cm)

TRAVEL PILLOW

MATERIALS
Super Bulky Weight Yarn:
  6$^1/_2$ ounces, 200 yards
    (180 grams, 183 meters)
Straight knitting needles, size 11 (8 mm) **or** size
  needed for gauge (*see Gauge, page 57*)
Yarn needle
Stitch markers - 2
16"w x 12"h (40.5 cm x 30.5 cm) Pillow form

GAUGE: In pattern, 10 sts = 3$^1/_2$" (9 cm);
        14 rows = 2$^3/_4$" (7 cm)

BODY (Make 2)
Cast on 43 stitches.

Rows 1-7: Knit each stitch across the row.

Row 8 (Right side): Knit 4 stitches, place a stitch marker on the right needle, knit 5 stitches, ★ purl 5 stitches, knit 5 stitches; repeat from ★ across to the last 4 stitches, place a stitch marker on the right needle, knit the last 4 stitches.

Row 9: Knit each stitch across to the first marker, purl each stitch across to the next marker, knit the last 4 stitches.

Row 10: Knit each stitch across to the first marker, knit 5 stitches, ★ purl 5 stitches, knit 5 stitches; repeat from ★ across to the next marker, knit the last 4 stitches.

Rows 11-14: Repeat Rows 9 and 10 twice.

Row 15: Knit each stitch across to the first marker, knit 5 stitches, ★ purl 5 stitches, knit 5 stitches; repeat from ★ across to the next marker, knit the last 4 stitches.

Row 16: Knit each stitch across the row, slipping the markers.

Rows 17-21: Repeat Rows 15 and 16 twice, then repeat Row 15 once **more**.

Row 22: Knit each stitch across to the first marker, knit 5 stitches, ★ purl 5 stitches, knit 5 stitches; repeat from ★ across to the next marker, knit the last 4 stitches.

Rows 23-49: Repeat Rows 9-22 once, then repeat Rows 9-21 once **more**, removing both markers on Row 49.

Rows 50-57: Knit each stitch across the row.

Bind off all stitches in **knit**.

FINISHING

With **wrong** sides of both pieces together, whipstitch along three sides *(Fig. 6, page 26)*. Insert pillow form and finish whipstitching the fourth side.

SCARF

Size	Finished Measurement
Small	5½" x 43" (14 cm x 109 cm)
Medium	6½" x 46½" (16.5 cm x 118 cm)
Large	7¼" x 50" (18.5 cm x 127 cm)

Size Note: Instructions are written for size Small with sizes Medium and Large in braces { }. Instructions will be easier to read if you circle all the numbers pertaining to your size. If only one number is given, it applies to all sizes.

MATERIALS

Medium/Worsted Weight Yarn:
4½{5½-7} ounces, 210{255-325} yards
130{160-200} grams, 192{233-297} meters
Knitting needles, size 8 (5 mm) **or** size needed
for gauge *(see Gauge, page 57)*
Stitch markers - 2
Yarn needle

GAUGE: In pattern, 17 stitches = 4" (10 cm);
24 rows = 3" (7.5 cm)

Gauge Swatch: 4" wide x 3" high
(10 cm x 7.5 cm)
Cast on 17 stitches.
Work same as Body for 24 rows.
Bind off all stitches in **knit**.

BODY

Cast on 23{27-31} stitches.

Rows 1-8: Knit each stitch across the row.

Row 9: Knit 4 stitches, place a stitch marker on the
right needle, purl each stitch across to the last
4 stitches, place a stitch marker on the right needle,
knit the last 4 stitches.

Instructions continued on page 44.

Row 10 (Right side): Knit each stitch across the row, slipping the markers.

Row 11: Knit each stitch across to the first marker, purl each stitch across to the next marker, knit the last 4 stitches.

Rows 12-20: Knit each stitch across the row, slipping the markers.

Row 21: Knit each stitch across to the first marker, purl each stitch across to the next marker, knit the last 4 stitches.

Repeat Rows 10-21 for pattern until Scarf measures approximately 42{45^1/$_2$-49}"/106.5{115.5-124.5} cm from cast on edge, ending by working Row 11 and removing both markers on last row worked.

Last 8 Rows: Knit each stitch across the row.

Bind off all stitches in **knit**.

HAT

Size	Finished Head Circumference
Small	16^1/$_4$" (41.5 cm)
Medium	17" (43 cm)
Large	18" (45.5 cm)

Size Note: Instructions are written for size Small with sizes Medium and Large in braces { }. Instructions will be easier to read if you circle all the numbers pertaining to your size. If only one number is given, it applies to all sizes.

MATERIALS
   Medium/Worsted Weight Yarn: **MEDIUM 4**
      3^1/$_2${4-4^1/$_2$} ounces, 165{185-210} yards
         100{110-130} grams, 151{169-192} meters
   Knitting needles, size 8 (5 mm) **or** size needed
      for gauge *(see Gauge, page 57)*
   Yarn needle

Note: Gauge is very important in this project *(see Gauge, page 57).*

GAUGE: In pattern, 17 stitches = 4" (10 cm);
            24 rows = 3" (7.5 cm)

Gauge Swatch: 4" wide x 3" high
                  (10 cm x 7.5 cm)
Cast on 17 stitches.
Work same as Body, page 46, for 24 rows.
Bind off all stitches in **knit**.

Instructions continued on page 46.

BODY

Cast on 69{73-77} stitches.

Rows 1-8: Knit each stitch across the row.

Row 9: Purl each stitch across the row.

Row 10 (Right side)**:** Knit each stitch across the row.

Row 11: Purl each stitch across the row.

Rows 12-20: Knit each stitch across the row.

Row 21: Purl each stitch across the row.

Row 22: Knit each stitch across the row.

Row 23: Purl each stitch across the row.

Rows 24-47: Repeat Rows 12-23 twice.

Rows 48-55: Knit each stitch across the row.

Row 56: Knit 8 stitches, knit 2 stitches together, ★ knit 11{12-13} stitches, knit 2 stitches together; repeat from ★ across to last 7 stitches, knit the last 7 stitches: you will now have 64{68-72} stitches.

Row 57: Purl each stitch across the row.

Row 58: Knit 7 stitches, knit 2 stitches together, ★ knit 10{11-12} stitches, knit 2 stitches together; repeat from ★ across to last 7 stitches, knit the last 7 stitches: you will now have 59{63-67} stitches.

Row 59: Purl each stitch across the row.

Rows 60-67: Knit each stitch across the row.

Row 68: Knit 6 stitches, knit 2 stitches together, ★ knit 9{10-11} stitches, knit 2 stitches together; repeat from ★ across to last 7 stitches, knit the last 7 stitches: you will now have 54{58-62} stitches.

46

Row 69: Purl each stitch across the row.

Row 70: Knit 6 stitches, knit 2 stitches together, ★ knit 8{9-10} stitches, knit 2 stitches together; repeat from ★ across to last 6 stitches, knit the last 6 stitches: you will now have 49{53-57} stitches.

Row 71: Purl each stitch across the row.

Rows 72-79: Knit each stitch across the row.

Row 80: Knit 5 stitches, knit 2 stitches together, ★ knit 7{8-9} stitches, knit 2 stitches together; repeat from ★ across to last 6 stitches, knit the last 6 stitches: you will now have 44{48-52} stitches.

Row 81: Purl each stitch across the row.

Row 82: Knit 5 stitches, knit 2 stitches together, ★ knit 6{7-8} stitches, knit 2 stitches together; repeat from ★ across to last 5 stitches, knit the last 5 stitches: you will now have 39{43-47} stitches.

Row 83: Purl each stitch across the row.

Rows 84-91: Knit each stitch across the row.

Row 92: Knit 4 stitches, knit 2 stitches together, ★ knit 5{6-7} stitches, knit 2 stitches together; repeat from ★ across to last 5 stitches, knit the last 5 stitches: you will now have 34{38-42} stitches.

Row 93: Purl each stitch across the row.

Row 94: Knit 4 stitches, knit 2 stitches together, ★ knit 4{5-6} stitches, knit 2 stitches together; repeat from ★ across to last 4 stitches, knit the last 4 stitches: you will now have 29{33-37} stitches.

Row 95: Purl each stitch across the row.

Rows 96-103: Knit each stitch across the row.

Row 104: Knit 3 stitches, knit 2 stitches together, ★ knit 3{4-5} stitches, knit 2 stitches together; repeat from ★ across to last 4 stitches, knit the last 4 stitches: you will now have 24{28-32} stitches.

Row 105: Purl each stitch across the row.

Row 106: Knit 3 stitches, knit 2 stitches together, ★ knit 2{3-4} stitches, knit 2 stitches together; repeat from ★ across to last 3 stitches, knit the last 3 stitches: you will now have 19{23-27} stitches.

Row 107: Purl each stitch across the row.

Rows 108-115: Knit each stitch across the row.

Row 116: Knit 2 stitches, knit 2 stitches together, ★ knit 1{2-3} stitch(es), knit 2 stitches together; repeat from ★ across to last 3 stitches, knit the last 3 stitches: you will now have 14{18-22} stitches.

Row 117: Purl each stitch across the row.

Instructions continued on page 48.

SIZE SMALL ONLY

Row 118: Knit 2 stitches together across the row: you will now have 7 stitches.

Row 119: Purl each stitch across the row.

Cut the working yarn, leaving a 36" (91.5 cm) end for sewing. See Finishing, page 49.

SIZE MEDIUM ONLY

Row 118: Knit 2 stitches, knit 2 stitches together, ★ knit 1 stitch, knit 2 stitches together; repeat from ★ across to last 2 stitches, knit the last 2 stitches: you will now have 13 stitches.

Row 119: Purl each stitch across the row.

Rows 120-127: Knit each stitch across the row.

Row 128: Knit 1 stitch, knit 2 stitches together across the row: you will now have 7 stitches.

Row 129: Purl each stitch across the row.

Cut the working yarn, leaving a 36" (91.5 cm) end for sewing. See Finishing, page 49.

SIZE LARGE ONLY

Row 118: Knit 2 stitches, ★ knit 2 stitches together, knit 2 stitches; repeat from ★ across: you will now have 17 stitches.

Row 119: Purl each stitch across the row.

Rows 120-127: Knit each stitch across the row.

Row 128: ★ Knit 1 stitch, knit 2 stitches together; repeat from ★ across to last 2 stitches, knit the last 2 stitches: you will now have 12 stitches.

Row 129: Purl each stitch across the row.

Row 130: Knit 2 stitches together across the row: you will now have 6 stitches.

Row 131: Purl each stitch across the row.

Cut the working yarn, leaving a 36" (91.5 cm) end for sewing. See Finishing, page 49.

Thread a yarn needle with the long end and insert it through the remaining stitches on the needle *(Fig. 11, page 36)*, removing the knitting needle. Pull the yarn tightly to close, then make a knot to secure the yarn. Do not remove the yarn needle and do not cut the yarn. Weave the seam *(Fig. 12, page 37)*. Once you get to the first row, make a knot to secure the yarn. Hide the yarn end by weaving through several inches in one direction and then weaving back in the opposite direction.

TASSEL

Cut a piece of cardboard 3" (7.5 cm) wide and as long as you want your finished tassel to be. Wind a double strand of yarn around the cardboard approximately 12 times. Cut an 18" (45.5 cm) length of yarn and insert it under all of the strands at the top of the cardboard; pull up **tightly** and tie securely. Leave the yarn ends long enough to attach the tassel. Cut the yarn at the opposite end of the cardboard and then remove it *(Fig. 16a)*. Cut a 6" (15 cm) length of yarn and wrap it **tightly** around the tassel twice, 1" (2.5 cm) below the top *(Fig. 16b)*; tie securely. Trim the ends.

Fig. 16a

Fig. 16b

TWISTED CORD

Cut one piece of yarn, 24" (61 cm) long or 3 times as long as the desired finished length. Insert one end through the top of the Tassel. Let someone hold one end with the Tassel near that end; twist the other end in the direction of the natural twist until it is **tight**. Bring the ends together, placing the Tassel at the folded end; let go of the Tassel and let the yarn twist around itself. Knot the end and attach it to the top of the Hat.

COLOR-BLOCK PULLOVER

Size	Finished Chest Measurement
4	24" (61 cm)
6	25$\frac{1}{2}$" (65 cm)
8	26$\frac{1}{2}$" (67.5 cm)
10	28$\frac{1}{2}$" (72.5 cm)
12	30" (76 cm)
14	32" (81.5 cm)
16	33" (84 cm)

SIZING

When choosing what size to make, you may want to measure a favorite sweater with similar styling and knit the size that has the nearest finished measurement. Once you have chosen a size, you may adjust the body length and the sleeve length to accommodate your actual measurements while adjusting the amount of yarn purchased accordingly.

Size Note: Instructions are written with sizes 4, 6, and 8 in the first set of braces { } and sizes 10, 12, 14, and 16 in the second set of braces { }. Instructions will be easier to read if you circle all the numbers pertaining to your size. If only one number is given, it applies to all sizes.

MATERIALS

Worsted/Medium Weight Yarn: MEDIUM 4

Color A (variegated)
{4$\frac{1}{2}$-5-5$\frac{1}{2}$}{6$\frac{1}{2}$-7$\frac{1}{2}$-8-9} ounces
{270-305-335}{395-455-485-545} yards
{130-140-160}{180-210-230-260} grams
{247-279-306}{361-416-443-498} meters

Color B (solid)
{4$\frac{1}{2}$-5-5$\frac{1}{2}$}{6$\frac{1}{2}$-7$\frac{1}{2}$-8-9} ounces
{270-305-335}{395-455-485-545} yards
{130-140-160}{180-210-230-260} grams
{247-279-306}{361-416-443-498} meters

Straight knitting needles, size 8 (5 mm) **or** size needed for gauge **(see Gauge, page 57)**

Straight pins or T-pins

Yarn needle

Note: Gauge is very important in this project **(see Gauge, page 57)**.

GAUGE: In Stockinette Stitch
(knit one row, purl one row);
18 stitches and 24 rows = 4" (10 cm)

BODY HALF

(Make 2 with Color A and 2 with Color B)

BOTTOM BAND

Cast on {29-31-32}{34-36-38-39} stitches.

Rows 1-10: Knit each stitch across the row.

BODY

Row 1: Purl each stitch across the row.

Row 2 (Right side)**:** Knit each stitch across the row.

Repeat Rows 1 and 2 for Stockinette Stitch until piece measures approximately {15$\frac{1}{2}$-17-18$\frac{1}{2}$}{19$\frac{1}{2}$-20$\frac{1}{2}$-21$\frac{1}{2}$-24}"/ {39.5-43-47}{49.5-52-54.5-61} cm from cast on edge, ending by working a **purl** row.

Bind off all stitches in **knit**.

SLEEVE
(Make 1 with Color A and 1 with Color B)

CUFF
Cast on {29-29-30}{30-31-31-31} stitches.

Rows 1-9: Knit each stitch across the row.

BODY
Row 1 (Right side)**:** Knit {9-9-6}{6-7-7-7} stitches, ★ increase in the next stitch (*Figs. 9a & b, page 32*), knit {9-9-7}{7-5-5-5} stitches; repeat from ★ across: you will now have {31-31-33}{33-35-35-35} stitches.

Row 2: Purl each stitch across the row.

Row 3 (Increase row)**:** Increase in the first stitch, knit each stitch across to the last stitch, increase in the last stitch: you will now have {33-33-35}{35-37-37-37} stitches.

Row 4: Purl each stitch across the row.

Row 5: Knit each stitch across the row.

Row 6: Purl each stitch across the row.

Row 7 (Increase row)**:** Increase in the first stitch, knit each stitch across to the last stitch, increase in the last stitch: you will now have {35-35-37}{37-39-39-39} stitches.

Repeat Rows 4-7, {11-12-13}{16-17-17-19} times: you will now have {57-59-63}{69-73-73-77} stitches.

Beginning with a **purl** row, work even (not increasing or decreasing) in Stockinette Stitch until Sleeve measures approximately {11$\frac{1}{2}$-12$\frac{3}{4}$-14}{15$\frac{1}{2}$-17-18$\frac{1}{2}$-19$\frac{1}{2}$}"/ {29-32.5-35.5}{39.5-43-47-49.5} cm from the cast on edge, ending by working a **purl** row.

Bind off all stitches in **knit**.

Instructions continued on page 52.

FINISHING

Most seams are joined with the **right** side of both pieces facing you. However, the Body Halves in this pullover are joined with the **wrong** side of both pieces facing you, forming a decorative ridge on the right side.

With **wrong** side of one Color A Body Half and one Color B Body Half facing, weave the seam to form the front (**Fig. 12, page 37**).

With **wrong** side of remaining Body Halves facing, and placing them on opposite sides as you did for the front, weave the seam to form the back.

With **right** side of front and back together, pin pieces together along the top edge. Sew the shoulder seams, beginning $\{2^1/_2\text{-}2^1/_2\text{-}2^3/_4\}\{2^3/_4\text{- }3\text{-}3\text{-}3\}$"/ $\{6.5\text{-}6.5\text{-}7\}\{7\text{-}7.5\text{-}7.5\text{-}7.5\}$ cm from center seams and ending at outer edge.

To mark Sleeve placement, measure $\{6\text{-}6^1/_2\text{-}7\}\{7^1/_2\text{-}8\text{-}8\text{-}8^1/_2\}$"/ $\{15\text{-}16.5\text{-}18\}\{19\text{-}20.5\text{-}20.5\text{-}21.5\}$ cm down from each shoulder seam and tie a small piece of contrasting color yarn on each side of front and back Body.

Fold the Color A Sleeve in half lengthwise to find the center of the bound off edge. With right sides together, pin the center of the Sleeve edge to the shoulder seam of Color B Body and the top corners of the Sleeve to the Body at markers. Pin the rest of the top of the Sleeve in place. Repeat with Color B Sleeve. Sew Sleeves in place.

Beginning at edge of Cuff on Sleeve, weave underarm seam and side seam of Body. Repeat for the second side.

One of the greatest joys of knitting is sharing your handmade projects with others … and **one of the greatest rewards** is sharing these projects with those who are in need. **You can encourage** children in your class to do this in several ways.

Warm Up America! is a foundation that co-ordinates the efforts of volunteers nationwide who knit and crochet afghans to help those in need. And, you don't have to belong to a formal group or club to participate.

Thousands and thousands of afghans each year are sent to hospitals, nursing homes, shelters, American Red Cross chapters, and other social services agencies. These basic patchwork afghans are made of forty-nine 7" x 9" rectangular sections that are sewn together. Any pattern stitch can be used for the rectangle, including the Dishcloth pattern shown on page 31. It can be made 7" x 9" by using acrylic worsted weight yarn and size 7 straight knitting needles **or** size needed to obtain the gauge of 5 sts to 1". **Encourage your students** to knit the rectangles and then get together for an "assembly party" to complete the afghan. **Volunteers** are asked to assemble and donate afghans in their own communities.

Warm Up America! is a program for **neighbors to help neighbors.**

For additional information, visit www.warmupamerica.com

As part of the **Precious Pals program**, dressed-up bears are given to children across the country who are facing a crisis. The Bear Hat and Scarf set, page 54, is designed to fit a small craft bear. Your students may knit the bear accessories and mail their dressed-up bear to:

The Knitting Guild of America,

P.O. Box 3388, Zanesville, Ohio 43702-3388.

Or, visit www.tkga.com for more information.

Urge your students **to knit** not only for themselves, but **for their communities — they'll be glad you did!**

BEAR'S HAT & SCARF SET

Finished Size: Hat - 4" tall x 9" around (10 cm x 23 cm)

MATERIALS

Medium/Worsted Weight Yarn:
Main Color (solid) - 1 ounce, 60 yards (30 grams, 55 meters) **total**
Contrasting Color (variegated) - 5 yards (4.5 meters) **total**
Straight knitting needles, size 8 (5 mm) **or** size needed for gauge (*see Gauge, page 57*)
Yarn needle
Crochet hook (to attach fringe)
10" Craft Bear

GAUGE: In Garter Stitch
(knit every row),
9 stitches and 22 rows = 2" (5 cm)

HAT

With Main Color, cast on 36 stitches.

Row 1: Knit each stitch across the row.

Row 2 (Right side)**:** Knit each stitch across the row.

Note: Place a small piece of yarn around any stitch to mark Row 2 as **right** side.

Repeat Row 2 until Hat measures approximately 4" (10 cm) from cast on edge, ending by working a **wrong** side row.

Next Row: Knit 2 stitches together across the row (*Figs. 10a & b, page 35*): you will now have 18 stitches.

Cut yarn, leaving a long end for sewing.

Thread a yarn needle with the yarn end and weave through the remaining stitches on the needle, pulling tightly to close; weave back seam (*Fig. 12, page 37*).

Weave in the yarn ends.

Fold edge of Hat back ¾" (19 mm) to right side.

POM-POM

Cut a piece of cardboard 2" (5 cm) square.
Wind Contrasting Color around the cardboard until it is approximately ½" (12 mm) thick in the middle (*Fig. 17a*).
Carefully slip the yarn off the cardboard and firmly tie an 18" (45.5 cm) length of yarn around the middle (*Fig. 17b*). Leave the yarn ends long enough to attach the pom-pom. Cut the loops on both ends and trim the pom-pom into a smooth ball (*Fig. 17c*).
Attach Pom-Pom to top of Hat.

Fig. 17a

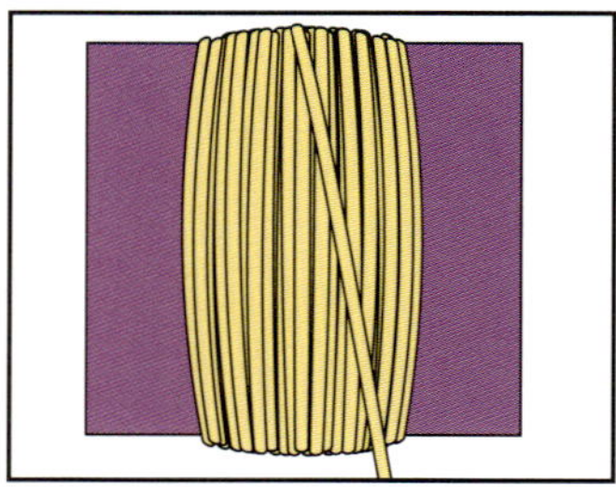

Fig. 17b

Fig. 17c

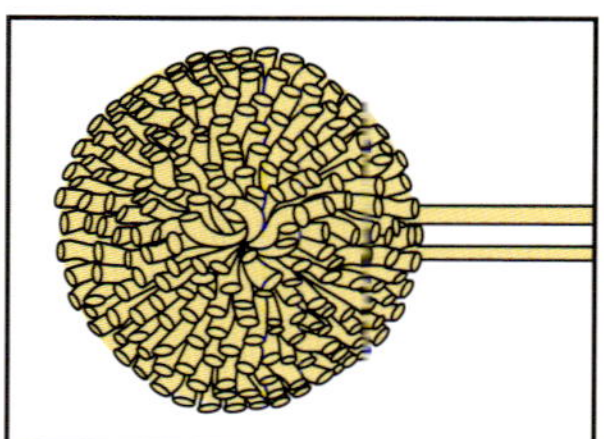

SCARF

With Main Color, cast on 6 stitches.

Knit each stitch across every row until Scarf measures approximately 14" (35.5 cm) from cast on edge.

Bind off all stitches in **knit**.

FRINGE

Cut a piece of cardboard 3" (7.5 cm) square. Wind Contrasting Color **loosely** and **evenly** around the cardboard until the card is filled, then cut across one end; repeat as needed.
Fold one strand in half.
With **wrong** side facing and using a crochet hook, draw the folded end up through a stitch and pull the loose ends through the folded end **(Fig. 18a)**; draw the knot up **tightly (Fig. 18b)**.
Add fringe in each stitch at each end of the Scarf. Lay the Scarf flat on a hard surface and trim the ends.

Fig. 18a

Fig. 18b

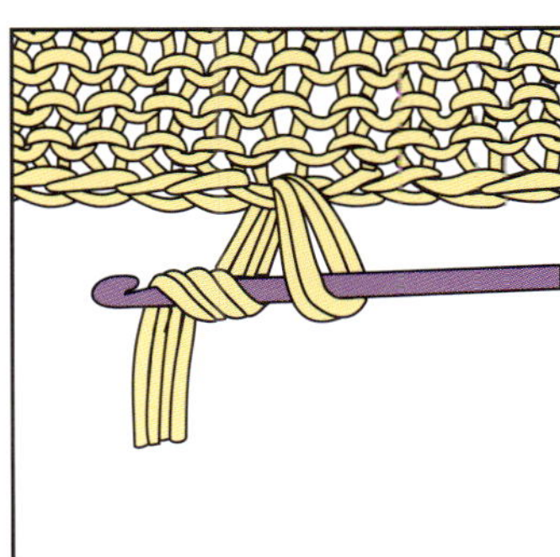

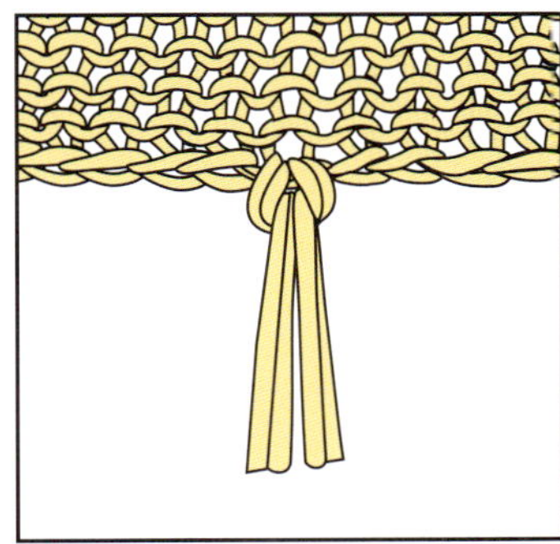

ADDITIONAL INFORMATION

Knit instructions are typically written using abbreviations, symbols, terms, and punctuation marks. Since this is a beginners' book, there are very few abbreviations used. However, here is a list of some common abbreviations, symbols, and terms used in knit books.

ABBREVIATIONS

CC	Contrasting Color
cm	centimeters
K	knit
MC	Main Color
mm	millimeters
P	purl
Rnd(s)	Round(s)
st(s)	stitch(es)
tog	together
YO	yarn over

TERMINOLOGY

U.S. and International terminologies are a little bit different:

U.S.		International
yarn over (YO)	=	yfwd or yrn
gauge	=	tension
bind off	=	cast off

SYMBOLS AND TERMS

★ — work all instructions following a ★ (star) as many **more** times as indicated in addition to the first time.

change to larger/smaller size needles — replace the right needle with the size needle specified and work the stitches from the left needle as instructed; at the end of the row, replace the left needle with the other size needle.

loosely — (casting on, adding new, or binding off stitches) the work should be as stretchy as the knitting.

right side vs. wrong side — the right side of your work is the side that will show when the piece is finished.

work even — work without increasing or decreasing in the established pattern.

Yarn Weight Symbol & Names	SUPER FINE 1	FINE 2	LIGHT 3	MEDIUM 4	BULKY 5	SUPER BULKY 6
Type of Yarns in Category	Sock, Fingering Baby	Sport, Baby	DK, Light Worsted	Worsted, Afghan, Aran	Chunky, Craft, Rug	Bulky, Roving

KNITTING NEEDLES																
U.S.	0	1	2	3	4	5	6	7	8	9	10	10½	11	13	15	17
U.K.	13	12	11	10	9	8	7	6	5	4	3	2	1	00	000	---
Metric - mm	2	2.25	2.75	3.25	3.5	3.75	4	4.5	5	5.5	6	6.5	8	9	10	12.75

■□□□ **BEGINNER**	Projects for first-time knitters using basic knit and purl stitches. Minimal shaping.
■■□□ **EASY**	Projects using basic stitches, repetitive stitch patterns, simple color changes, and simple shaping and finishing.
■■■□ **INTERMEDIATE**	Projects with a variety of stitches, such as basic cables and lace, simple intarsia, double-pointed needles and knitting in the round needle techniques, mid-level shaping and finishing.
■■■■ **EXPERIENCED**	Projects using advanced techniques and stitches, such as short rows, fair isle, more intricate intarsia, cables, lace patterns, and numerous color changes.

PUNCTUATION

When reading knitting instructions, read from punctuation mark to punctuation mark. Just as in reading, commas (,) and semicolons (;) mean pause.

colon (:) — the number(s) given after a colon at the end of a row tells the number of stitches you should have on that row. When repeating rows, the number given is for the last row.

parentheses ( ) or brackets [ ] — indicate a repetition, so you should work the instructions within the ( ) or [ ] **as many** times as it says. Information given in parentheses or brackets may also explain more about the pattern.

braces { } — contains information pertaining to multiple sizes.

WHAT IS GAUGE?

Gauge is the number of stitches and rows per inch or centimeters and is used to determine the finished size of a project. Most knitting patterns specify the gauge that you must match to make sure your project fits right and that you'll have enough yarn to complete your project.

Before beginning most knitted items, it's absolutely necessary for you to knit a sample swatch in the pattern stitch with the weight of yarn and needle size suggested. The swatch must be large enough for you to measure your gauge, usually a 4" (10 cm) square. After completing the swatch, measure it. If your swatch is larger or smaller than specified, make another, changing needle size to get the correct gauge.

Remember, DO NOT HESITATE TO CHANGE NEEDLE SIZE IN ORDER TO OBTAIN CORRECT GAUGE. Once you have obtained correct gauge, you should continue to measure the total width of your work every 3-4" (7.5-10 cm) to be sure your gauge does not change.

For many of the projects in this book, gauge doesn't really matter that much. The Bookmarks and the Coasters can certainly be a little bigger or smaller without changing the overall effect. However, most knit patterns specify the gauge that you must match.

DROPPED STITCHES

A dropped stitch is a stitch that accidentally slips off the needle and may easily unravel more than one row. To fix a dropped stitch, hold the work with the knit side facing in Stockinette Stitch *(knit one row, purl one row)* or with a purl stitch below the last loop in Garter Stitch *(knit every row) (Fig. 19a)*. Insert a crochet hook through the loop of the dropped stitch, hook the strand of yarn immediately above it *(Fig. 19b)*, and pull it through the loop on your hook. Continue in this manner until you have used all of the strands of yarn, turning the work after every strand when working in Garter Stitch only. Slip the stitch onto the left needle with the right side of the stitch to the front.

Fig. 19b

Fig. 19a

YARN INFORMATION

Each project in this leaflet was made with medium/worsted weight or super bulky weight yarn. **Any brand of yarn** in the specified weight may be used. It is best to refer to the yardage/meters when determining how many balls or skeins to purchase. **Remember**, to arrive at the finished size, it is the **GAUGE/TENSION that is important**, not the brand of yarn.

For your convenience, listed below are the specific yarns used to create our photography models.

BOOKMARKS
Bernat® Handicrafter® Cotton
#10 French Blue
#43 Forest Green
#54 Grape
#89 Banana Yellow
#13131 Celadon
#13132 Pumpkin
Lion Brand® Lion Cotton
#146 Fuchsia

WRIST BANDS & SWEAT BANDS
Red Heart® Super Saver®
#0971 Camouflage
Bernat® Satin
#05733 Bermuda

NAPKIN RINGS
Bernat® Handicrafter® Christmas
#920 Mistletoe Tinsel

DISHCLOTH
Lion Brand® Lion Cotton
#146 Fuchsia

COASTER
Bernat® Handicrafter® Cotton
#54 Grape

JUGGLING BALLS
Bernat® Handicrafter® Cotton
#89 Banana Yellow
#16 Red
EPI Peaches & Creme
#175 Fiesta Ombre

LAP ROBE
Lion Brand® Wool-Ease Chunky
#147 Boysenberry

TRAVEL PILLOW
Lion Brand® Wool-Ease Chunky
#147 Boysenberry

BOY'S HAT & SCARF SET
Bernat® Satin
#05109 Seaswell

GIRL'S HAT & SCARF SET
Bernat® So Soft®
#76792 Pow Wow

COLOR-BLOCK PULLOVER
Red Heart® Kids™
Solid - #2360 Orchid
Variegated - #2955 Dream Girl

BEAR'S HAT & SCARF SET
Red Heart® Kids™
Solid - #2360 Orchid
Variegated - #2955 Dream Girl

INDEX

Production Team: Instructional Editor - Sarah J. Green; Technical Editor - Cathy Hardy; Editorial Writer - Kimber Ross; Graphic Artist - Mandy L. Hickman; Senior Graphic Artist - Rebecca J. Hester; Photo Stylists - Karen Hall and Cassie Newsome; and Photographers - Lloyd Litsey and Andrew Paul Uilkie.

We have made every effort to ensure that these instructions are accurate and complete. We cannot, however, be responsible for human error, typographical mistakes, or variations in individual work.

Items made and instructions tested by Raymelle Greening and Margaret Taverner.

©2004 by Leisure Arts, Inc., 5701 Ranch Drive, Little Rock, AR 72223. All rights reserved. This publication is protected under federal copyright laws. Reproduction or distribution of this publication or any other Leisure Arts publication, including publications which are out of print, is prohibited unless specifically authorized. This includes, but is not limited to, any form of reproduction or distribution on or through the Internet, including posting, scanning, or e-mail transmission.